Dynamic Bitmap Graphics with PHP and gd

Dynamic Bitmap Graphics with PHP and gd

Jacek Artymiak

Second Edition

Lublin

Dynamic Bitmap Graphics with PHP and gd, Second Edition
by Jacek Artymiak

Published by:
devGuide.net Jacek Artymiak

email: *phpgd-ed-02@devguide.net*
www: *http://www.devguide.net*

First edition 2003
Second edition 2007

Printed in the USA

07 10 9 8 7 6 5 4 3 2

ISBN-13: 978-8-3916-6516-9

Printed by Lightning Source, Inc. on behalf of devGuide.net

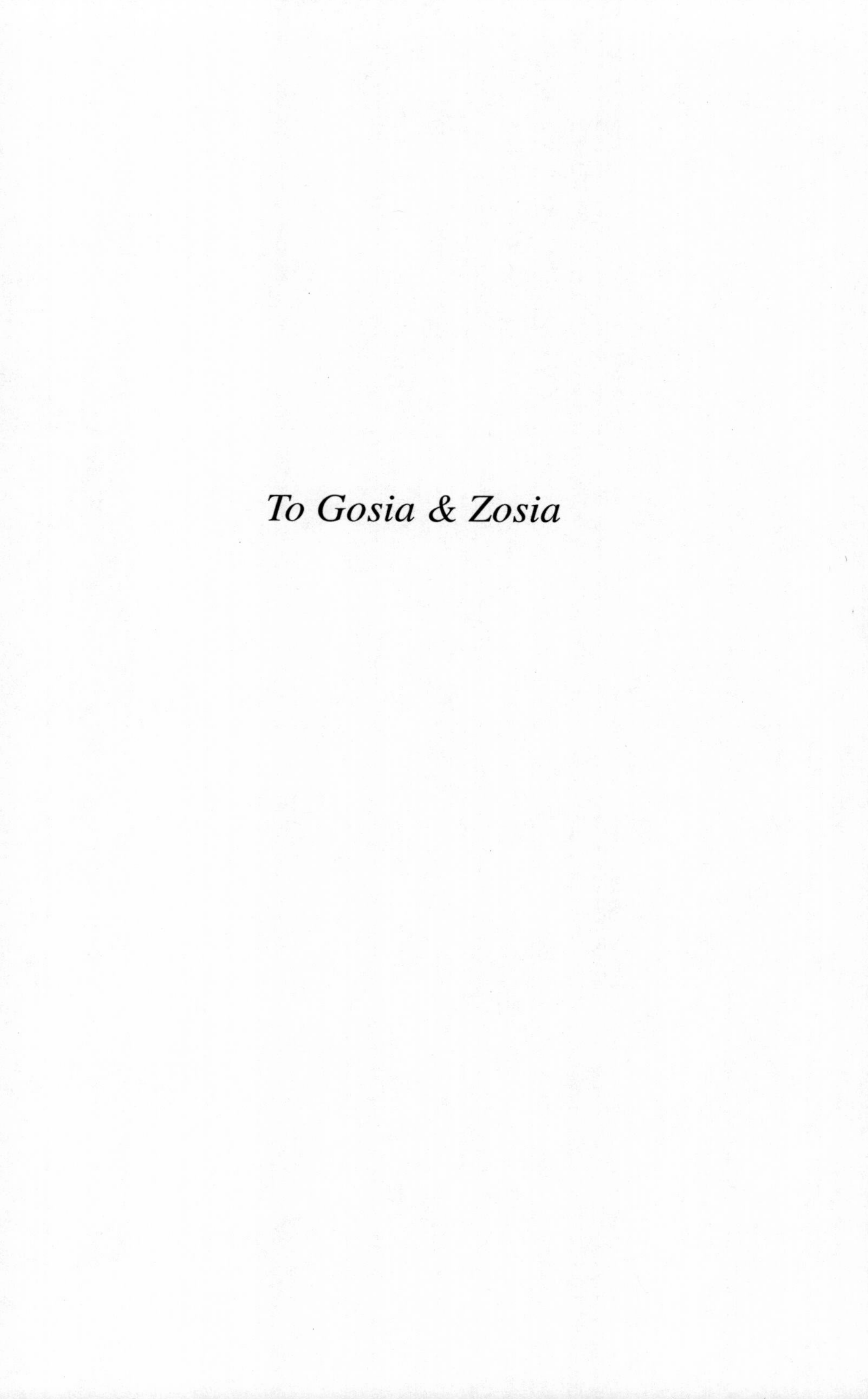

To Gosia & Zosia

About This Book

A picture is worth a thousand words, especially when it is used to illustrate business, financial, or scientific data. It is worth even more, if you can generate it on demand and serve the latest information in the visual format.

If your job requires writing PHP applications that generate bitmap images on the fly, then this book will teach you how to do it using PHP and the excellent gd library from Thomas Boutell.

Some of you might remember that I wrote the first edition of this book as a tutorial for the IBM *developerWorks* website in 2003. And although what I wrote then is still (mostly) true nowadays, it's been high time for a new edition. The GIF support in gd is back, and there are new versions of PHP and Apache to choose from. So, here it is, improved and as easy to follow as before.

Have fun!

Jacek Artymiak

January 7, 2007
Lublin, Poland

This page intentionally left blank

Table of Contents

About This Book vii

Table of Contents ix

Chapter 1: Before You Start 1

1.1: Why You Should Read This Book? 1
1.2: Objectives 1
1.3: System Requirements 2
1.4: Tips for Assembling a Working PHP System 3
1.5: Building Required Tools from Sources 4
1.6: Additional Tools 5
1.7: Using a PHP-Enabled Hosting Service 7
1.8: Testing Your PHP/gd Installation 7

Chapter 2: First Steps 11

2.1: Start with the Right Header 11
2.2: Prepare Your Canvas 12
2.3: Compose Your Palette 12
2.4: Prepare the Background 13

Chapter 3: GD Drawing Primitives 15

3.1 Having Fun with Pixels 15

Chapter 4: Basic Data Visualization 17

4.1 Make a Clock with Arcs and Lines 17
4.2 Visualizing Numeric Data 20
4.3 Add Some Text 22

Chapter 5: Before You Send Your Masterpiece to the Visitor ... 27

5.1 Decide What Type of Image You Want to Generate 27

Chapter 6: Embedding Images in HTML/XHTML Documents ... 29

Appendix A: Resources 31

Appendix B: Reader Support 33

Index 35

Colophon 39

Chapter 1

Before You Start

1.1 Why You Should Read This Book?

A picture is worth a thousand words, especially when it is used to illustrate business, financial, or scientific data. It is worth even more if it can be generated on demand, so it can present the latest information in compact visual format. If your job requires writing such applications in PHP, then this book will teach you how to generate bitmap images using PHP and the gd library.

1.2 Objectives

By the end of this book, you will be able to start writing your own scripts to generate bitmap images using PHP and the gd library. You will be prepared to apply that knowledge to illustrate business, financial, and scientific data. Specifically, you will learn:

- Basics on setting up your PHP/gd system.
- Operating system-specific tips to facilitate setting up your own system.
- How-tos for testing your PHP/gd installation.
- Steps to prepare your canvas, color palette, and background fill/image.
- A primer on gd drawing primitives.
- Exercises to help data-visualization results.
- Tips for choosing a file format.
- Instructions to embed your script into XHTML documents.

1.3 System Requirements

You need:

- Access to a 'good' operating system. I consider the following operating systems good for learning, testing, and deployment:
  - **Free/Net/OpenBSD**: all excellent choices for development and production systems.
  - **Linux**: another fine choice; if you are new to this system, try the Ubuntu Linux Server and choose the LAMP installation profile.
  - **Apple Mac OS X**: a popular choice among geeks.
  - Other Unix-like operating systems are also acceptable as long as they can run the following pieces of software:
    - **Apache**: choose the version you need and read the documentation at *http://httpd.apache.org/docs/*. Both 1.x.x and 2.x.x versions work with PHP, so it is up to you to decide what you need.
    - **PHP**: choose the branch you want to follow, 4.x.x, 5.x.x, or 6.x.x and visit this URL for installation tips:

      http://www.php.net/manual/en/installation.php
    - **gd 2.0.33**: you can find the current gd documentation at this URL:

      http://www.boutell.com/gd/manual2.0.33.html
  - **Microsoft Windows NT/2000/XP/Vista**: if you must...
- A machine with:
  - Processor clocked at 100 MHz or more.
  - 32 MB of RAM or more. Of course, that 32 MB is the bare minimum, big enough for embedded systems, too small for comfortable development work. If you will be deploying a site that makes heavy use of gd, get as much RAM as possible.
  - A 500-MB of free hard disk space if you want to install the system, PHP, and your code. The more the merrier, as always.

Using the Apache HTTPD server is not compulssory, you can use a different HTTP server like lighttpd, thttpd, Zeus, IdeaWebServer, Caudium, and others as long as it is supported by PHP, or it supports PHP, whoever has the bigger ego these days (for the list of officially suppored HTTP servers, read *http://www.php.net/manual/en/installation.php*). On top of that, the gd library will need the following support libraries: freetype2, zlib, libpng, and libjpeg6.

1.4 Tips for Assembling a Working PHP System

The easiest way to put together a working PHP setup for the purposes of following the examples in this book (and in many cases, for production use) is to use pre-compiled Apache, PHP, gd, and any additional libraries that gd may require. This is especially easy nowadays since PHP code is distributed with an enhanced version of gd code, which means that you don't have to download and build as much code as 2–3 years ago.

The following is a list of installation tips for some of the most popular operating systems:

- **FreeBSD**. Use the ports system to install the latest versions of Apache and PHP software. Then, install gd and other required libraries. The ports installation scripts can spot missing libraries and install them when necessary. The official FreeBSD ports documentation is available from:

  http://www.freebsd.org/doc/en_US.ISO8859-1/books/handbook/ports.html

- **Linux**. This varies from distribution to distribution. But, since you can install any distribution you like, try the latest Ubuntu Linux Server installation CD-ROM and choose the LAMP installation profile. It's the easiest way to get started with Linux, Apache, MySQL, and PHP. At the end of the installation you'll have all of the tools you'll need. Ubuntu Linux is here:

  http://www.ubuntu.com

- **Apple Mac OS X**. **Apache** Apache is a part of the default installation, so you only need to start it and add PHP and the rest of the software. Apple offers a nice page with detailed installation instructions:

  http://developer.apple.com/internet/opensource/php.html

- **NetBSD**. Use the packages system, which is similar to FreeBSD ports.

  http://www.mclink.it/personal/MG2508/nbsdeng/chap-pack.html

- **OpenBSD**. Apache is a part of the default installation, so you only have to download PHP and the rest of the software, which you can do with `pkg_add php4-core-4.x.x.tgz` and `pkg_add php4-gd-4.x.x.tgz` If you want to know more about PHP4 extension packages for OpenBSD, install and read `php4-extensions-4.x.x.tgz` Package names for PHP5 start with the `php5-*` prefix. After you're done installing PHP and the gd extensions, start Apache with `apachectl start` (must be done by the superuser) and you're set. If you are new to OpenBSD packages, read *The Ports and Packages collection* page of the OpenBSD project's web site:

  http://www.openbsd.org/ports.html
  http://www.openbsd.org/4.0_packages/

- **Microsoft Windows**. You have a choice of either Microsoft's own IIS or Apache. Apache, PHP, gd and the rest of the necessary libraries are also available as a binary distributions with GUI installers from these sites:

  http://www.apache.org/dist/httpd/binaries/win32/
  http://www.php.net/downloads.php/

- **Other operating systems**. Either use pre-compiled packages or build software from sources.

1.5 Building Required Tools from Sources

If you cannot find ready-made binaries for your system, you will have to build them from sources using an ANSI C/C++ compiler like GCC. As for the sources of particular packages, you can find them on the Internet:

Apache: *http://www.apache.org/dist/httpd/*

PHP: *http://www.php.net/downloads.php/*

gd: *http://www.boutell.com/gd/*

libpng: *http://www.libpng.org/pub/png/libpng.html*

zlib: *http://www.gzip.org/zlib/*

libjpeg: *http://www.ijg.org/*

freetype2 (optional, required for rendering TrueType fonts):
http://www.freetype.org/

t1lib (optional, required for rendering Type 1 fonts):
http://freshmeat.net/projects/t1lib/

For details on building every package, see README or INSTALL files found in each package. You should build in the following order:

1. zlib
2. libpng
3. libjpeg6
4. freetype2
5. t1lib
6. gd
7. Apache
8. PHP

Most of these tools can be built by following the standard Unix routine:

```
$ ./configure
$ ./make
$ sudo ./make install
```

1.6 Additional Tools

Additional software required to test your scripts includes a graphical Web browser. Ideally, it ought to be running on a machine other than the one generating graphics, so you can check whether your scripts are accessible to the outside world. All major browsers (Mozilla, Internet Explorer, Opera, and others) are able to handle such tasks. You will also need a plain text editor. In this case vi (or vim), emacs, TextPad, or BBEdit work equally well.

PHP Version 4.4.4

System	Linux bomberman 2.4.32-grsec+f6b+gr217+nfs+a32+fuse23+tg+++opt+c8+gr2b-v6.194 #1 SMP Tue Jun 6 15:52:09 PDT 2006 i686
Build Date	Nov 7 2006 12:56:47
Configure Command	'./configure' '--with-apxs=/dh/apache/template/bin/apxs' '--with-mysql=/usr' '--enable-calendar' '--enable-memory-limit' '--enable-exif' '--with-config-file-path=/etc/php' '--enable-trans-sid' '--with-curl=/usr' '--with-mcrypt=/usr' '--without-pear' '--with-gd' '--with-ttf=/usr' '--with-freetype-dir=/usr' '--with-jpeg-dir=/usr' '--with-png-dir=/usr' '--with-zlib-dir=/usr' '--with-openssl=/usr' '--enable-mbstring=all'
Server API	Apache
Virtual Directory Support	disabled
Configuration File (php.ini) Path	/etc/php/php.ini
PHP API	20020918
PHP Extension	20020429
Zend Extension	20050606
Debug Build	no
Zend Memory Manager	enabled
Thread Safety	disabled
Registered PHP Streams	php, http, ftp, https, ftps, compress.zlib

gd

GD Support	enabled
GD Version	bundled (2.0.28 compatible)
FreeType Support	enabled
FreeType Linkage	with freetype
GIF Read Support	enabled
GIF Create Support	enabled
JPG Support	enabled
PNG Support	enabled
WBMP Support	enabled
XBM Support	enabled

1.7 Using a PHP-Enabled Hosting Service

Nothing wrong with that. In fact, it is the easiest way to get started. The only drawback being the fact that most inexpensive hosting plans don't let you configure your PHP setup.

Just check if they offer support for gd and how complete is it. Is it just plain gd, or do they also support TrueType and Type 1 libraries? You might have to dig around the official site, check the F.A.Qs, etc.

For example, Dreamhost.com has a page of PHP setup reports at *http://php.dreamhosters.com/*.

1.8 Testing Your PHP/gd Installation

When you have all required components installed, you can check if the support for gd is working. This is done with two simple scripts. First, you create a general PHP test script:

```
<?php phpinfo(); ?>
```

Save the script as *chapter-01-php-info-test.php* (remember to save it in the XHTML document directory), change file access modes to read-only for all users with `chmod 0444 test.php` and request the script using the browser (for example, *http://localhost/chapter-01-php-info-test.php*. You should see a long table listing various PHP options. Do a search for *gd* and check for the `--with-gd` option and the *gd* section (support for gd ought to be enabled). You should see the sections shown on the left.

If the browser reports errors, check the configuration of your HTTP server, PHP, and gd and try again. Next, create a test script called *chapter-01-test-chart.php*:

```
<?php header("Content-Type: image/jpeg");

 # Set the dimensions of the canvas
 $cw = 500;
 $ch = 300;

 # Create canvas
 $c = ImageCreate($cw, $ch);
```

```
 # Generate color palette
 for ($n = 0; $n <= 255; $n++) {
  $cols[$n] = ImageColorAllocate($c, $n, $n, $n);
 }

 # Create background
 ImageFilledRectangle($c, 0, 0, 600, 400,
                      $cols[255]);

 # Display all characters in a font
 $font = 4;
 $dx = ImageFontWidth($font);
 $dy = ImageFontHeight($font);
 $x = ($cw / 2) - (16 * $dx);
 $y = ($ch / 2) - (4 * $dy);
 $m = 0;
 $z = 0;

 for ($n = 0; $n <= 7; $n++) {
  for ($m = 0; $m <= 31; $m++) {
   ImageChar($c, $font, $x + $dx * $m, $y,
             chr($z), $cols[0]);
   $z++;
  }
  $y = $y + $dy;
 }

 # Draw a nice thin border around the edges of
 # the image
 ImageRectangle($c, 0, 0, $cw-1, $ch-1, $cols[0]);

 # Generate image
 ImageJPEG($c);
?>
```

Again, you need to make this script readable by all users, and request it using your browser. The result should be identical to the following:

```
◆▒␉␌␍␊°±␤␋┘┐┌└┼⎺⎻─⎼⎽├┤┴┬│≤≥π≠£·
 !"#$%&'()*+,-./0123456789:;<=>?
@ABCDEFGHIJKLMNOPQRSTUVWXYZ[\]^_
`abcdefghijklmnopqrstuvwxyz{|}~

 Ą˘Ł¤ĽŚ§¨ŠŞŤŹ-ŽŻ°ą˛ł´ľśˇ¸šşťź˝žż
ŔÁÂĂÄĹĆÇČÉĘËĚÍÎĎĐŃŇÓÔŐÖ×ŘŮÚŰÜÝŢß
ŕáâăäĺćçčéęëěíîďđńňóôőö÷řůúűüýţ˙
```

This page intentionally left blank

Chapter 2

First Steps

2.1 Start with the Right Header

Once you complete the initial tests, it is time to write your own gd scripts. To do that, you need to learn about the general structure of a gd script. I'll start with the basics. Every script that generates graphics must start with this command:

```
header("Content-Type: image/jpeg");
```

Using the `header()` function, you can set the value of the HTTP headers sent by the HTTP server to the HTTP client (your Web browser). One of these headers is `Content-Type`, which informs the HTTP client what kind of data it is about to receive. The client uses that information to decide how it should process the data it receives. It may decide to use external converters or display information that it is unable to handle on its own.

For example, `image/jpeg` informs the client that it will receive a bitmap image in the JPEG format. The client can now decide what to do with this image—decode it, use an external viewer, or give up and tell the user that it is unable to display this particular type of image. Advanced web browsers let the user define what should happen on the user's end of the connection.

After the `Content-Type` header is sent to the browser, your script can do whatever job you designed it for. Remember, however, that the only output your script can produce is the bytestream that makes up the image. This rules out the use of commands like echo or print to generate XHTML code within the same script.

But what if you want to generate an XHTML document that contains a dynamically generated image? You'll learn how you can do it later in this book, but before I get to that, you need to learn how to generate a bitmap image.

2.2 Prepare Your Canvas

Before you begin drawing anything, you need to prepare the canvas you'll paint on. This is done with a call to the `ImageCreate()` function:

```
# Set the dimensions of the canvas
$cw = 500;
$ch = 300;

# Create canvas
$c = ImageCreate($cw, $ch);
```

The numeric ID returned by `ImageCreate()` is used by all commands that modify the image. This creates an interesting possibility to create two or more separate images in the same script.

However, the practical use of this feature is limited because the script can only send a single image to the HTTP client that invokes it. On the other hand, as you will see later on, it is possible to combine two or more images or save images to the local disk (on the server).

Note that the dimensions of the canvas ought to match the dimensions of the image specified in the `height` and `width` attributes of the `<img />` tag. If you use different values, the image still displays in the browser's window, but it is distorted. It is not a particularly good design trick, so it is best to avoid it.

2.3 Compose Your Palette

Now it is time to mix some virtual paint. Although gd 2.x.x can work with a palette of millions of colors, you will probably limit the size of the palette to 256 colors because that is the number of colors *both* the 1.8.4 and the 2.x.x releases of gd can work with. This approach is safe if you cannot control the PHP/gd configuration on the server you'll be deploying your scripts to.

Every color in the palette is created with a call to the `ImageColorAllocate()` function, which takes four arguments: the position of the given color in the palette and the values of the red, green, and blue components (their values are integers in the 0..255 range). For example, the following piece of code creates a gray-scale palette:

```
# Generate color palette
for ($n = 0; $n <= 255; $n++) {
 $cols[$n] = ImageColorAllocate($c, $n, $n, $n);
}
```

If you are not sure how many colors you'll need, don't worry. You do not have to define the whole palette at once and you can modify it later in the script, but defining it at the beginning is more elegant.

It is also very easy to change your mind. To re-define a color, simply use `ImageColorAllocate()` with the same canvas ID and color ID, but with different R, G, and B color values. You can also remove a color from the palette with `ImageColorDeAllocate()` like this:

```
ImageColorDeAllocate($c, $cols[7]);
```

2.4 Prepare the Background

You are now ready to begin creating your masterpiece. You are free to use any technique you like, but remember that once you draw something, it cannot be undone, so the order in which you draw your image is important.

Therefore, the first thing to do is paint the canvas using a solid color or an imported image. The first method is shown in the following example:

```
# Create Background
ImageFilledRectangle($c, 0, 0, 499, 299,
                     $cols[255]);
```

Since there is no special function to create the background, use the `Image-FilledRectangle()` function, which draws a filled rectangle on the canvas, a rectangle whose ID is given as the first argument. The next four values are coordinates of the upper left and the lower right corners of the rectangle. The last argument is the fill-color ID (from the palette created earlier).

Of course, `ImageFilledRectangle()` can be used to draw filled rectangles at any other time, and not only to create a solid background. You might also use the `ImageRectangle()` function, which draws an empty rectangle with a single-pixel border; it takes exactly the same arguments as `ImageFilledRectangle()` Note that gd places the origin in the upper left corner of the image and then grows leftward and downward.

The second method, creating a background from an existing file, can be achieved with these functions:

- `ImageCreateFromGD()`
- `ImageCreateFromGD2()`
- `ImageCreateFromGD2Part()`
- `ImageCreateFromGIF()`
- `ImageCreateFromJPEG()`
- `ImageCreateFromPNG()`
- `ImageCreateFromString()`
- `ImageCreateFromWBMP()`
- `ImageCreateFromXBM()`
- `ImageCreateFromXPM()`

The arguments of these functions can be either the access paths to local files or URLs of files (static or generated dynamically) downloaded from remote servers. The second way of accessing files creates a particularly interesting opportunity to write scripts that download dynamically updated images (satellite photos, news images, and so forth) and add your own commentary, enrich with additional information, or combine with other images.

Such tricks work better if you install gd 2.x.x, as it can handle a palette larger than 256 colors. This avoids nasty surprises when someone on the other end changes the palette they are using.

Note that the file format you use to create an image canvas does not determine the format of the output file; this is decided at the time you send the image to the browser. Also, when you import an image, you may need to know its size; this can be done with `GetImageSize()` For more information on these functions, see the *Image* section in the PHP function library documentation.

Chapter 3

GD Drawing Primitives

3.1 Having Fun with Pixels

Once the background is ready, you can begin drawing whatever you like using these functions:

- `ImageSetPixel()`
- `ImageLine()`
- `ImageDashedLine()`
- `ImageRectangle()`
- `ImageFilledRectangle()`
- `ImagePolygon()`
- `ImageFilledPolygon()`
- `ImageArc()`
- `ImageFilledArc()`

The first of these functions, `ImageSetPixel()`, simply draws a single pixel. It only needs four arguments: canvas ID, X and Y coordinates, and the color ID. You can use it to add detail to your images or use the `random()` function, as I did in the following example:

```
<?php header("Content-Type: image/jpeg");

 # Set the dimensions of the canvas
 $cw = 200;
 $ch = 200;

 # Create canvas
 $c = ImageCreate($cw, $ch);

 # Generate color palette
 for ($n = 0; $n <= 255; $n++) {
  $cols[$n] = ImageColorAllocate($c, $n, $n, $n);
 }
```

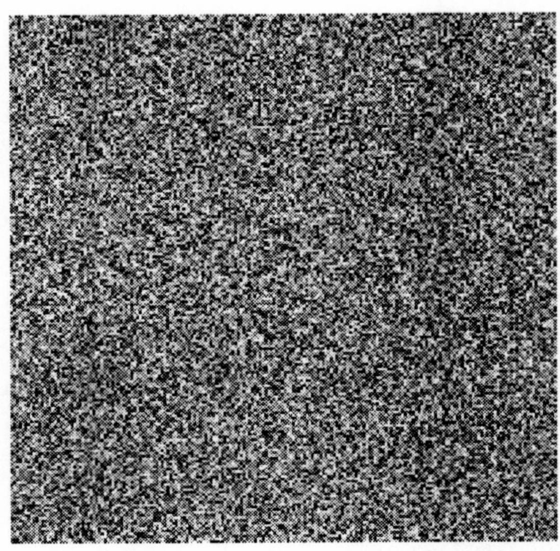

```
 # Create background
 ImageFilledRectangle($c, 0, 0, $cw, $ch, $cols[255]);

 # Draw some ellipses, circles, and arcs
 for ($n = 0; $n < $cw; $n++) {
  for ($m = 0; $m < $ch; $m++) {
   ImageSetPixel($c, $n, $m, (int) rand(0, 255));
  }
  $m = 0;
 }

 # Generate image
 ImageJPEG($c);
?>
```

The above script generates a random pixel map, shown in the image above.

Chapter 4

Basic Data Visualization

4.1 Make a Clock with Arcs and Lines

While random pixel maps are cute to look at, they're not very useful (except for the Computer Graphics people, who like to use them as 'bump maps' for generating rough 3D surfaces). A much more interesting example would be one that shows how to use gd for visualization of numeric real-time data.

I'll use the current time (you cannot get more real-time than this) to create a clock which shows the time it was generated on the server. This clock is a very good starting point for showing how to use `ImageArc()`, `ImageLine()`, and `ImageDashedLine()` functions.

```
<?php header("Content-Type: image/jpeg");

 # Set the dimensions of the canvas
 $cw = 300;
 $ch = 300;

 # Create canvas
 $c = ImageCreate($cw, $ch);

 # Generate color palette
 $cols[0] = ImageColorAllocate($c, 0, 0, 0);
 $cols[1] = ImageColorAllocate($c, 255, 255, 255);
 $cols[2] = ImageColorAllocate($c, 255, 0, 0);
 $cols[3] = ImageColorAllocate($c, 0, 255, 0);
 $cols[4] = ImageColorAllocate($c, 0, 0, 255);
 $cols[5] = ImageColorAllocate($c, 255, 0, 255);

 # Create background
 ImageFilledRectangle($c, 0, 0, $cw - 1, $ch - 1,
                      $cols[1]);
```

```
# Compute coordinates of the center of the image
$x = (int) $cw / 2;
$y = (int) $ch / 2;

# Draw the circular border
ImageArc($c, $x, $y, (int) ($cw * .9),
         (int) ($ch * .9), 0, 360, $cols[0]);

# Read local time
$t = localtime();

# Initialize hour, minute, and second variables
$th = $t[2];
$tm = $t[1];
$ts = $t[0];

# Convert hour from 24- to 12 hour format
if ($th > 11) {
 $th -= 11; }

# Prepare some constants
$hi = deg2rad(30);
$mi = deg2rad(6);
$adj = deg2rad(90);

# Compute coordinates of the hour, minute,
# and second hands
# Compute angles
$th = $hi * $th - $adj;
$tm = $mi * $tm - $adj;
$ts = $mi * $ts - $adj;

# Compute the length and the coordinates of
# the hour hand
$hhl = $cw * 0.15;
$hhx = $hhl * cos($th);
$hhy = $hhl * sin($th);

# Compute the length and the coordinates of
# the minute hand
$mhl = $cw * 0.25;
$mhx = $mhl * cos($tm);
$mhy = $mhl * sin($tm);
```

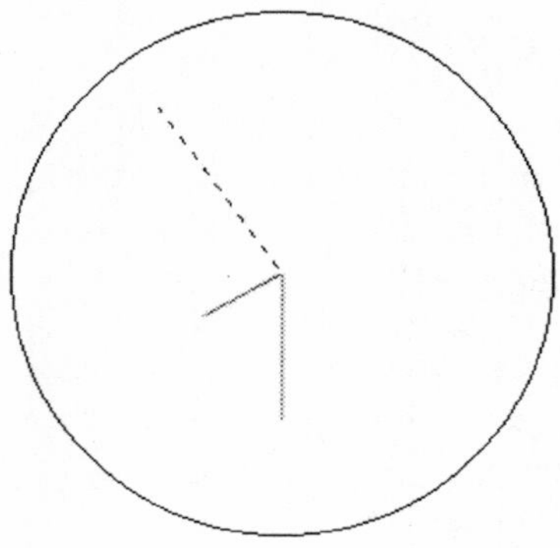

```
  # Compute the length and the coordinates of
  # the second hand
  $shl = $cw * 0.35;
  $shx = $shl * cos($ts);
  $shy = $shl * sin($ts);

  # Draw the hour hand
  ImageLine($c, $x, $y, $x + $hhx, $y + $hhy, $cols[2]);

  # Draw the minute hand
  ImageLine($c, $x, $y, $x + $mhx, $y + $mhy, $cols[3]);

  # Draw the second hand
  ImageDashedLine($c, $x, $y, $x + $shx, $y + $shy,
                  $cols[4]);

  # Generate image
  ImageJPEG($c, '', 100);
?>
```

Now, every time you reload the script, you see an analog clock showing the local server time, which might be different from your local time.

Making changes required to display local time at the visitor's place is left as an exercise to the reader. The results of running the clock script can be seen in the figure above.

4.2 Visualizing Numeric Data

The clock example above was an interesting introduction to the subject of data visualization, but its business or scientific use is a bit limited. A more useful example of data visualization could be a plot of results of surveys conducted in different geographic locations.

For the purposes of this example, I'll assume that I asked developers in California, Texas, and New York to tell me what desktop manager they use, and I want to present the results on a map of the USA. This is exactly what the following script does.

```
<?php header("Content-Type: image/jpeg");

 # Set the dimensions of the canvas
 $cw = 300;
 $ch = 300;

 # Define chart-drawing function
 function drawChart($c, $cx, $cy, $v1, $v2, $v3,
                    $c0, $c1, $c2, $c3) {
  ImageFilledRectangle($c, $cx, $cy - $v1,
                       $cx + 10, $cy, $c1);
  ImageRectangle($c, $cx, $cy - $v1,
                 $cx + 10, $cy, $c0);
  ImageFilledRectangle($c, $cx + 5, $cy - $v2,
                       $cx + 15, $cy, $c2);
  ImageRectangle($c, $cx + 5, $cy - $v2,
                 $cx + 15, $cy, $c0);
  ImageFilledRectangle($c, $cx + 10, $cy - $v3,
                       $cx + 20, $cy, $c3);
  ImageRectangle($c, $cx + 10, $cy - $v3,
                 $cx + 20, $cy, $c0);
 }

 # Map displacement values
 $mdx = 0;
 $mdy = 0;

 # Make array of map points
 $usa[0] = 30 + $mdx; $usa[1] = 50 + $mdy;
```

```
$usa[2] = 15 + $mdx; $usa[3] = 90 + $mdy;
$usa[4] = 40 + $mdx; $usa[5] = 130 + $mdy;
$usa[6] = 85 + $mdx; $usa[7] = 135 + $mdy;
$usa[8] = 120 + $mdx; $usa[9] = 170 + $mdy;
$usa[10] = 130 + $mdx; $usa[11] = 140 + $mdy;
$usa[12] = 180 + $mdx; $usa[13] = 125 + $mdy;
$usa[14] = 200 + $mdx; $usa[15] = 160 + $mdy;
$usa[16] = 215 + $mdx; $usa[17] = 165 + $mdy;
$usa[18] = 195 + $mdx; $usa[19] = 105 + $mdy;
$usa[20] = 210 + $mdx; $usa[21] = 70 + $mdy;
$usa[22] = 200 + $mdx; $usa[23] = 60 + $mdy;
$usa[24] = 215 + $mdx; $usa[25] = 15 + $mdy;
$usa[26] = 195 + $mdx; $usa[27] = 10 + $mdy;
$usa[28] = 165 + $mdx; $usa[29] = 50 + $mdy;
$usa[30] = 105 + $mdx; $usa[31] = 55 + $mdy;
$usa[32] = 95 + $mdx; $usa[33] = 45 + $mdy;

# Create canvas
$c = ImageCreate($cw, $ch);

# Generate color palette
$cols[0] = ImageColorAllocate($c, 0, 0, 0);
$cols[1] = ImageColorAllocate($c, 255, 255, 255);
$cols[2] = ImageColorAllocate($c, 255, 0, 0);
$cols[3] = ImageColorAllocate($c, 0, 255, 0);
$cols[4] = ImageColorAllocate($c, 0, 0, 255);
$cols[5] = ImageColorAllocate($c, 255, 255, 0);

# Create background
ImageFilledRectangle($c, 0, 0, $cw - 1, $ch - 1,
                     $cols[1]);

# Draw map
ImageFilledPolygon($c, $usa, 17, $cols[3]);

# Draw map outline
ImagePolygon($c, $usa, 17, $cols[0]);
drawChart($c, 190, 100, 80, 70, 55, $cols[0], $cols[4],
          $cols[2], $cols[5]);
```

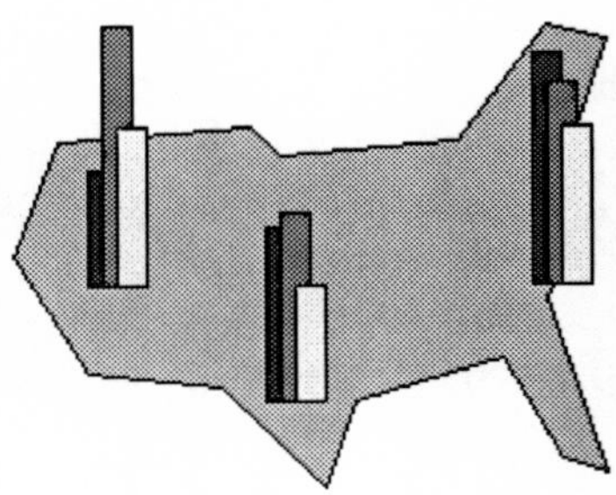

```
 drawChart($c, 100, 140, 60, 65, 40, $cols[0], $cols[4],
          $cols[2], $cols[5]);
 drawChart($c, 40, 100, 40, 90, 55, $cols[0], $cols[4],
          $cols[2], $cols[5]);

 # Generate image
 ImageJPEG($c);
?>
```

The result looks like the image above. Note that in this script, I wrote a simple function for drawing charts, `drawChart()`, to make my life easier.

You should do the same when you are performing a similar type of visualization. This way, over time you build a library of handy functions for drawing various types of charts. The map of the USA shown in this example is a very rough approximation and does not include Alaska or Hawaii. Making it look better is left as an exercise to the reader.

The map is drawn using `ImagePolygon()` and `ImageFilledPolygon()`, which both expect an array of coordinates arranged in the *x0*, *y0*, *x1*, *y1*, ... order, so the number of the array elements is twice the number of the points in the polygon. But remember to give these functions the number of points, not the number of array elements.

4.3 Add Some Text

The previous example does a good job of turning numbers into a picture, but it could benefit from at least some basic text. This can be done with the `ImageString()` (for horizontal text) and `ImageStringUp()` (for vertical text) functions. Both expect the following arguments: canvas ID, font ID, X and Y coordinates, text string, and color ID. The font ID is an integer in the 1..5 range (specifying one of the five built-in bitmap fonts). The following script shows how to use these functions in practice. It is an extended version of the previous script.

```
<?php header("Content-Type: image/jpeg");

 # Set the dimensions of the canvas
 $cw = 300;
 $ch = 300;

 # Define chart-drawing function
 function drawChart($c, $cx, $cy, $v1, $v2, $v3,
                    $c0, $c1, $c2, $c3) {
  ImageFilledRectangle($c, $cx, $cy - $v1,
                       $cx + 10, $cy, $c1);
  ImageRectangle($c, $cx, $cy - $v1,
                 $cx + 10, $cy, $c0);
  ImageFilledRectangle($c, $cx + 5, $cy - $v2,
                       $cx + 15, $cy, $c2);
  ImageRectangle($c, $cx + 5, $cy - $v2,
                 $cx + 15, $cy, $c0);
  ImageFilledRectangle($c, $cx + 10, $cy - $v3,
                       $cx + 20, $cy, $c3);
  ImageRectangle($c, $cx + 10, $cy - $v3,
                 $cx + 20, $cy, $c0);
 }

 # Map displacement values
 $mdx = 0;
 $mdy = 0;

 # Make array of map points
 $usa[0] = 30 + $mdx; $usa[1] = 50 + $mdy;
 $usa[2] = 15 + $mdx; $usa[3] = 90 + $mdy;
 $usa[4] = 40 + $mdx; $usa[5] = 130 + $mdy;
 $usa[6] = 85 + $mdx; $usa[7] = 135 + $mdy;
 $usa[8] = 120 + $mdx; $usa[9] = 170 + $mdy;
 $usa[10] = 130 + $mdx; $usa[11] = 140 + $mdy;
 $usa[12] = 180 + $mdx; $usa[13] = 125 + $mdy;
```

```
$usa[14] = 200 + $mdx; $usa[15] = 160 + $mdy;
$usa[16] = 215 + $mdx; $usa[17] = 165 + $mdy;
$usa[18] = 195 + $mdx; $usa[19] = 105 + $mdy;
$usa[20] = 210 + $mdx; $usa[21] = 70 + $mdy;
$usa[22] = 200 + $mdx; $usa[23] = 60 + $mdy;
$usa[24] = 215 + $mdx; $usa[25] = 15 + $mdy;
$usa[26] = 195 + $mdx; $usa[27] = 10 + $mdy;
$usa[28] = 165 + $mdx; $usa[29] = 50 + $mdy;
$usa[30] = 105 + $mdx; $usa[31] = 55 + $mdy;
$usa[32] = 95 + $mdx; $usa[33] = 45 + $mdy;

# Create canvas
$c = ImageCreate($cw, $ch);

# Generate color palette
$cols[0] = ImageColorAllocate($c, 0, 0, 0);
$cols[1] = ImageColorAllocate($c, 255, 255, 255);
$cols[2] = ImageColorAllocate($c, 255, 0, 0);
$cols[3] = ImageColorAllocate($c, 0, 255, 0);
$cols[4] = ImageColorAllocate($c, 0, 0, 255);
$cols[5] = ImageColorAllocate($c, 255, 255, 0);

# Create background
ImageFilledRectangle($c, 0, 0, $cw - 1, $ch - 1,
                     $cols[1]);

# Draw map
ImageFilledPolygon($c, $usa, 17, $cols[3]);

# Draw map outline
ImagePolygon($c, $usa, 17, $cols[0]);
drawChart($c, 190, 100, 80, 70, 55, $cols[0], $cols[4],
          $cols[2], $cols[5]);
drawChart($c, 100, 140, 60, 65, 40, $cols[0], $cols[4],
          $cols[2], $cols[5]);
drawChart($c, 40, 100, 40, 90, 55, $cols[0], $cols[4],
          $cols[2], $cols[5]);

# GNOME
ImageFilledRectangle($c, 60, 203, 70, 210, $cols[2]);
```

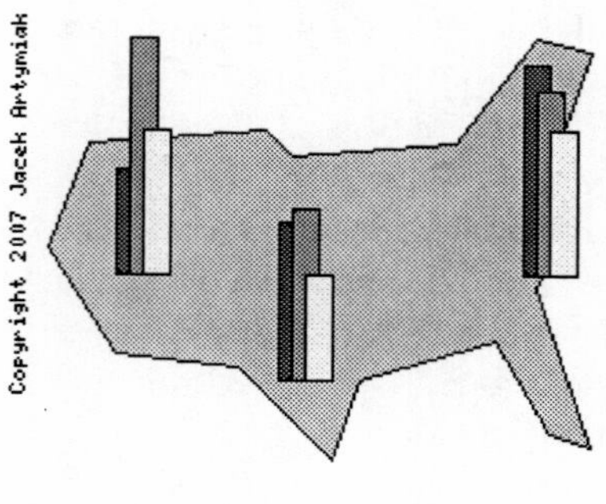


```
 ImageRectangle($c, 60, 203, 70, 210, $cols[0]);
 ImageString($c, 2, 75, 200, "GNOME", $cols[0]);

 # KDE
 ImageFilledRectangle($c, 120, 203, 130, 210, $cols[4]);
 ImageRectangle($c, 120, 203, 130, 210, $cols[0]);
 ImageString($c, 2, 135, 200, "KDE", $cols[0]);

 # GNUStep
 ImageFilledRectangle($c, 165, 203, 175, 210, $cols[5]);
 ImageRectangle($c, 165, 203, 175, 210, $cols[0]);
 ImageString($c, 2, 180, 200, "GNUStep", $cols[0]);

 # Copyright info
 ImageStringUp($c, 1, 0, 145,
               "Copyright 2002 Jacek Artymiak",
               $cols[0]);

 # Generate image
 ImageJPEG($c);
?>
```

The image at the top of this page shows the result you get from running this script.

The built-in bitmap fonts are always available, but if you'd like to use other fonts, you have to install the freetype2 library and use the `ImageFTText()` function to display text strings using the chosen TrueType font.

You can also use PostScript Type 1 fonts if you install the t1lib library; in this case, you use the `ImagePSLoadFont()` and `ImagePSText()` functions. In both cases, gd and PHP need to be built with support for these libraries.

Note that Type 1 fonts take longer to render than TrueType fonts; this may lead to script timeouts. You can solve the timeout problem by running your script on faster hardware or by adjusting the script timeout limit (default 30 seconds). Learn more about related functions in the *Image* section of the PHP function documentation.

Chapter 5

Before You Send Your Masterpiece to the Visitor

5.1 Decide What Type of Image You Want to Generate

So far, you have generated JPEG images, but you may also generate images in the PNG and WBMP (used in WAP-enabled devices such as mobile phones) formats. To do this, replace `ImageJPEG()` with `ImagePNG()` or `ImageWBMP()`. If you do that, don't forget to replace

```
header("Content-Type: image/jpeg");
```

with

```
header("Content-Type: image/png");
```

or, with

```
header("Content-Type: image/vnd.wap.wbmp");
```

If you give `ImageJPEG()`, `ImagePNG()`, or `ImageWBMP()` file access paths as the second attribute, they save the image to the file instead of sending it to the browser.

Chapter 6

Embedding Images in HTML/XHTML Documents

So far, to invoke the scripts in this book, you call them directly, which is not the most convenient way of accessing the images they generate. What if you wanted to integrate them into an HTML/XHTML page? That is actually quite easy. All you have to do is place the URL of the script that generates the image into the `src` argument of the `<img />` tag:

```
<html>
<head>
    <title>gd book</title>
</head>
<body>
    <p><img src="chapter-04-clock.php" />
       <img src="chapter-04-usa.php" /></p>
</body>
</html>
```

And here is the resulting image:

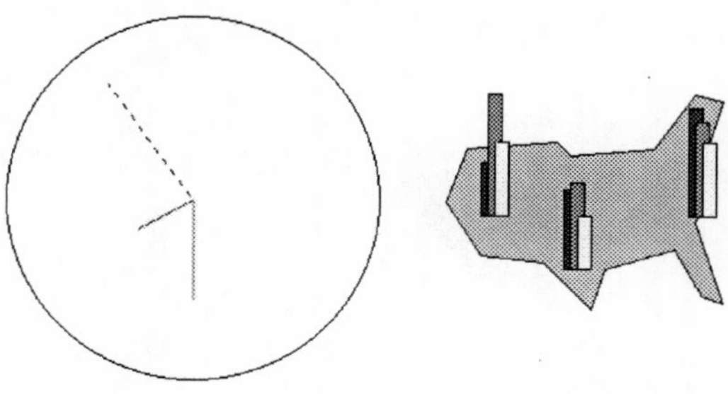

Appendix A
Resources

- gd documentation:
  - *http://www.boutell.com/gd/manual2.0.33.html*
- Apache documentation:
  - *http://httpd.apache.org/docs/*
- Additional information for developers using PHP in *Programming PHP, Second Edition* by Kevin Tatroe, Rasmus Lerdorf, and Peter MacIntyre. Published by O'Reilly Media, 2006
  - *http://www.oreilly.com/catalog/progphp2/*
- For help on learning programming Web applications with PHP, see *Web Database Applications with PHP and MySQL, Second Edition* by Hugh E. Williams and David Lane. Published by O'Reilly and Associates, 2004
  - *http://www.oreilly.com/catalog/webdbapps2/*
- For a general discussion of information visualization, read the Edward R. Tufte's trilogy available from Graphics Press: *The Visual Display of Quantitative Information, 2001; Envisioning Information, 1990;* and *Visual Explanations: Images and Quantities, Evidence and Narrative, 1997*
  - *http://www.edwardtufte.com/tufte/*
- For Mac OS X users, Apple offers instructions on adding PHP
  - *http://developer.apple.com/internet/opensource/php.html*
- Download the installation manual for PHP
  - *http://www.php.net/manual/en/installation.php*

- The gd library needs the following additional support libraries: freetype2 (TrueType font support), zlib, libpng, libjpeg6, t1lib (Type 1 font support:
  - *http://freetype.sourceforge.net/*
  - *http://www.zlib.net/*
  - *http://www.libpng.org/pub/png/libpng.html*
  - *http://www.ijg.org/*
  - *ftp://sunsite.unc.edu/pub/Linux/libs/graphics/*
- PHP, gd, and the rest of the necessary libraries are also available as a binary distribution with a GUI installer
  - *http://www.php.net/downloads.php*
- Feel free to experiment with other functions from the *Image* section of the PHP function libraries.
  - *http://www.php.net/manual/en/ref.image.php*
- For Microsoft Windows, if you don't have IIS installed, you need to install the Apache binaries
  - *http://www.apache.org/dist/httpd/binaries/win32/*

Appendix B
Reader Support

This book, like others from devGuide.net has its own support page with links, files, and screenshots. Visit us at *http://www.devguide.net*.

Index

Apache HTTPD server vii, 2–5, 32
  documentation 31
apachectl 4
Apple Mac OS X 2–3, 31
arcs 17

background 1, 13
BBEdit 5
Boutell, Thomas vii

C/C++ 4
canvas 1
Caudium 3
chmod 7
color palette 12–14
configure 5
Content-Type 7, 11, 15, 17, 20, 23, 27
cos() 18–19

data visualization of 1, 17, 20, 22
David Lane 31
deg2rad() 18
Dreamhost.com 7

Edward R. Tufte 31
emacs 5

file
  access mode 7
  format 1, 14

fonts
  TrueType 7, 25–26, 32
  Type 1 7, 26, 32
FreeBSD
  operating system 3–4
  ports 3–4
freetype2 3, 5, 25, 32

GCC 4
gd
  1.8.4 12
  2.0.33 2
  2.x.x 12, 14
  documentation 31
  drawing primitives 1
  installation 7
  library vii, 1, 3–5, 7, 11–13, 15, 17, 26, 32
  setting up 1
  testing 1
GetImageSize() 14
GIF vii
gray-scale palette 12

header() 7, 11, 15, 17, 20, 23, 27
HTML 29
  embedding scripts inside 1, 29
HTTP client 3, 7, 11–12
Hugh E. Williams 31
IdeaWebServer 3

ImageArc() 15, 17–18
ImageChar() 8
ImageColorAllocate() 8, 12–13, 15, 17, 21, 24
ImageColorDeAllocate() 13
ImageCreate() 7, 12, 15, 17, 21, 24
ImageCreateFromGD() 14
ImageCreateFromGD2() 14
ImageCreateFromGD2Part() 14
ImageCreateFromGIF() 14
ImageCreateFromJPEG() 14
ImageCreateFromPNG() 14
ImageCreateFromString() 14
ImageCreateFromWBMP() 14
ImageCreateFromXBM() 14
ImageCreateFromXPM() 14
ImageDashedLine() 15, 17–19
ImageFTText() 25
ImageFilledArc() 15
ImageFilledPolygon() 15, 21–22, 24
ImageFilledRectangle() 8, 13, 15–17, 20–21, 23–25
ImageFontHeight() 8
ImageFontWidth() 8
ImageJPEG() 8, 16, 18–19, 22, 25, 27
ImageLine() 15, 17–19
ImagePNG() 27
ImagePSLoadFont() 26
ImagePSText() 26
ImagePolygon() 15, 21–22, 24
ImageRectangle() 8, 13, 15, 20, 23, 25
ImageSetPixel() 15–16
ImageString() 22, 25
ImageStringUp() 22, 25
ImageWBMP() 27
image, size of 14
image/jpeg 7, 11, 15, 17, 20, 23, 27
image/png 27
image/wbmp 27
<img /> 12, 29
  height 12
  src 29
  width 12
installation 3

JPEG 11, 27

Kavin Tatroe 31

LAMP 2–3
Lane, David 31
Lerdorf, Rasmus 31
libjpeg6 3, 5, 32
libpng 3–5, 32
lighttpd 3
lines 17
Linux
  operating system 2–3
  Ubuntu 2–3
localtime() 18

MacIntyre, Peter 31
Mac OS X 2–3, 31
make 5
make install 5
Microsoft 4
  IIS 4, 32
  Internet Explorer 5
  Windows 2, 4, 32

Windows *cont.*
2000 2
NT 2
Vista 2
XP 2
mobile phones 27
Mozilla 5
MySQL 3, 31

NetBSD
operating system 4
packages 4

OpenBSD
operating system 4
packages 4
ports 4
Opera 5
operating systems
Apple Mac OS X 2–3, 31
FreeBSD 2–4
Linux 2–3
Microsoft Windows 2, 4, 32
NetBSD 2, 4
OpenBSD 2, 4
setting up 1
origin 13

palette 1
PHP vii, 1–5, 7, 12, 14, 26, 31–32
4.x.x 2, 4
5.x.x 2, 4
6.x.x 2
GUI Installer 32
HTTP server support in 3
hosting service 7
installation 7, 31
options 7

PHP *cont.*
`-with-gd` 7
script timeout 26
setting up 1
testing 1
Peter MacIntyre 31
`phpinfo()` 7
`pkg_add` 4
PNG 27
PostScript 26

Rasmus Lerdorf 31
`random()` 15
render 1
requirements 2
disk space 2
memory 2
processor 2

script timeout 26
`sin()` 18–19

t1lib 5, 26, 32
Tatroe, Kevin 31
TextPad 5
text 22, 25
editor 5
Thomas Boutell vii
thttpd 3
TrueType fonts 7, 25–26, 32
Tufte, Edward R. 31
Type 1 fonts 7, 26, 32

URL 14, 29
Unix 2, 5

vi 5
vim 5

WAP 27
web browser 5, 7–8, 11–12, 14, 27
WBMP 27
Williams, Hugh E. 31

XHTML 7, 11, 29
  embedding scripts inside 1, 29

Zeus 3
zlib 3, 5, 32

Colophon

Keeping with the tradition of getting as close to the processor core as possible, this book too was created using standard open source tools born in the UNIX environment and available for many popular commercial and free implementations of UNIX.

The manuscript was created on a variety of computers running Linux, OpenBSD, and Microsoft Windows. As he always does, the author used the *vi(1)* text editor to create and edit the manuscript. Every source file that this book was created from is stored in a CVS repository. Spelling was (hopefully) improved with the help of the immortal *ispell(1)*.

The layout of this book was implemented in *groff(1)*, a free implementation of *troff* (originally by Joseph F. Ossanna) written by James Clark and currently maintained by Werner Lemberg. Fonts used in this book are as standard as they get and come from the default set of fonts found in every implementation of *groff(1)*. All figures published in this book were created using PHP/gd, displayed in the *Mozilla Firefox* web browser and captured using *SnagIt 8*. Final PostScript and PDF files were generated with *groff(1)*, *gs(1)*, and *gv(1)*.

The cover image was captured with a Nokia N70 smartphone one evening autumn of 2006 in Lublin Poland. Afterwards, the image was transfered to Adobe Photoshop and incorporated into the final cover design.

LaVergne, TN USA
19 October 2009

161280LV00007B/174/A